New Life Clarity Publishing

205 West 300 South, Brigham City, Utah 84302
Http://newlifeclarity.com/

The Right of Ron Britton to be identified as the author of the work has been asserted by him in accordancewith the Copyright Act 1988.

New Life Clarity Publishing
name has been established by NLCP CORP.

All Rights Reserved.
No part of this publication may be reproduced, distributed, or transmitted in any form or by any means, including photocopying, recording, or other electronic or mechanical methods without the prior and express written permission of the author or publisher, except in the case of brief quotations embodied in critical reviews and certain other noncommercial uses permitted by copyright law.

Printed in the United States of America

ISBN- 979-8-3493-2866-4

Copyright@2024 Ron Britton

Gold Silver & Copper

The Transformation of Her Perception

Table of Content

1. Man Action 1
2. Colors Compliment 2
3. Sunset 3
4. Blue Moments 4
5. Fires 5
6. Beyond What I Know 6
7. You and I 7
8. 1st Quotes 8
9. 2nd Quotes 9
10. I Remember 11
11. Don't Force It 12
12. This Latina 13
13. In the Eyes Of 14
14. Revolutionary 15
15. Reflection 16
16. Like Chocolate 17
17. Bittersweet 18
18. Silent Killer 19
19. Beyond Recognition 20
20. Time! 21
21. Created in Love 22
22. Her Other Self 23
23. Hidden In 24
24. If Walls Could Talk 25
25. Crossroad 27

26.	Be Happy	28
27.	Living Without Regret	29
28.	The Touch	30
29.	Coffee	31
30.	Pink Infidelity	32
31.	What If?	33
32.	Beyond My Limits	34
33.	Vanilla Jones	35
34.	How Did I?	36
35.	We Dipped	37
36.	I Beheld	38
37.	Stop Falsifying	39
38.	Kit Cat Scratch Itch	40
39.	I Wish	41
40.	Better Than	42
41.	Dream	43
42.	I Want To	44
43.	Stained	45
44.	I Bet	46
45.	Antithesis	47
46.	Cold Winters	48
47.	Stains	49
48.	Moment	50
49.	Somethings	51
50.	No Smoke	52
51.	Cold Piece	53
52.	Fleeting Memory	54
53.	Finest Moment	55
54.	?	56
55.	After Thought	57
56.	Just Maybe	58
57.	Serial Lover	59
58.	My Soul	60
59.	Sugar Free	61
60.	Chances	62

61.	Until Forever	63
62.	Why?	64
63.	The Voice from The Womb	65
64.	Is It Real	66
65.	They Got the Hooch	67
66.	Sunshine	68
67.	Transfusion	69
68.	Just Say No!	70
69.	Living for A Memory	71
70.	It Just Looks Bad	72
71.	Never Return	73
72.	Deep Side of Love	74
73.	Ticking Time	75
74.	My Greatest	76
75.	Somebody Else	77
76.	Green Cat Eyes	78
77.	The Reward Outweigh the Risk	79
78.	Tomorrow	80
79.	My Alkebulan	81
80.	Samurai Love	82
81.	Tombstone	83
82.	The Light	84
83.	One Away	85
84.	Long Journey from Home	86
85.	Her Touch	87
86.	Night Breeze	88
87.	Like Honey	89
88.	Lovin Without Cost	90
89.	Caught Between Two Worlds	91
90.	Alienation Love	92
91.	Covenant or Contract	93
92.	Play The Hand	94
93.	The Chameleon	95
94.	Face to Face	96
95.	Living In Exile	97

96. I See with My Hands...98
97. Beyond..99
98. Orange Love 100
99. Who Are You?..101
100. How Can You Say!..102
101. Handwriting on The Wall 103
102 Imprisoned..104

1

Man Action

Man action is the act of a man protecting his woman from all the unnecessary, nonsensical acts that come from having past toxic relationships, causing momentary problems due those unhealthy friendships not being properly being cut off when they expired. At times, it's vital that many with a potentially good relationship, due to a collateral damage assessment to reduce as much harm as possible. Relationships are built on the health or the sickness level of relationships that's been tried by time and trials of afflictions from broken people who never got help for their trauma. If women, whose been in domestic relationships in the past doesn't take time to get heal and free themselves of the madness of wounds and abuses will not be able to embrace the love of a gentleman when he tries to protect and cover her, she will begin to perceive him as the predator from the last dead association. Every man is a protector by nature and that for some it comes only natural for him, can become a chore within itself, if not understood as love not harm. It should be mandated that couples, before engaging into a serious relationship that parties should evaluate whether the relationship is a long term, a fright by night or an alliance compatibility. Man action.

Colors Compliment

There's something beautiful about two distinct opposite colors. They at times can contradict one another and be polar crashing, non-matching from condescending worlds at war, but opposites can also just as true. There are many collaborating colors that supplement one another when matched side by side. They bring out the best in each other as if they were always meant to be. At times, I can see the beauty in two separate colors that blend their reflections to reveal a deeper essence of what togetherness is really supposed to be. The world has not learned the lesson in combining separate but equals hues of magnificent dimensions exposing the revelation of fluidity. Black and white create grayish color that allows uncertainty without always having to be perfect or always right. Red and white create a softer side of gentleness pink, more of a tenderness towards each other. Black and yellow are mixed as one unity, you get a representation of flush green evolving life that gives us a good feeling. When mixing colors amazing opposite colors together you always create something different, but beautiful. It's never a problem when two to three mixing colors together, only when mixing ethics, culture and traditions that we can't see the beauty in blended colors. Colors compliment

3

Sunset

She was my sunset, rising in the morning and settling during the evening tide. She was my life and death, breathing into me the will to live, yet killing me gently with the whispers of innuendos of truth. She knew how to flow with the streams of living water, floating right by my side as a life preserver, coaching me down through the turbulences of relationships. As the captain of my soul, as she led me through sessions of euphoric revelation, alighting my heart. As the sunset daily, as my mentor she taught me the essences of loving for a lifetime with endless periods of unconditional love without false expectations. She is both my revelation and illumination, as if the sun exploded into a burning star out of control, wandering through the universe without a guide. My sun will never rise nor ever set until I've drank a portion of her life-giving elixir. Sunset.

4

Blue Moments

Blue is bluesy because I'm feeling you in the zone of everlasting freedom. You have redeemed my space of time; you're always floating through my mind. Girl, you know you so, so fine. Like a glass of fine wine, you calm my winter storms and return me back to a place that's normal. Blue moments take me deep deeper into the depts of your revelations, which inflates my ability to see you as you really are, amazing. You grassed my soul with lush green pasture of life, and you know that's right. Blue moments are a reminder that life moves in ebbs and flows, shaking my heart to the core of interstellar galactic vibes. You set the tones and atmosphere of living in the here and now, pulling on me like a **black** hole with endless possibilities. Blue moments bring out the alites of my reality. Blue moments.

5

Fires

In my dreams, my nights are filled with blazing heat of inferno fires burning through the dark season of day. The fires burn with fervent temperatures of uncontrollable restraint as my heart is for you. You're my cloud by day and my pillar fire by night to guide me to the land of promise. Your love is unconditionally always ready to forgive and heal my wounded heart. My heart's desires have grown like the ambers of a blazing sun without restraint, consuming everything it it's path. As I mediated upon Your endless mercy I can't but lift Your name is praise for the rest of my days. I've never known a love so pure and true without ulterior motives. Your love will stand the test of time, none can compare to essences of Your existences. Your total sum of love and love through Your acts of continue provisions of all my needs being met daily. You're my portion. No reality can change my actuality of the peace You bring to the very revelation revealed from the scales that fell from my eyes. I see you as you are. Fires.

6

Beyond What I Know

Beyond what I know is a mystery of the unknown, therefore, there is more to know. I see things I cannot explain, but my curiously asks questions, seeking answers. There is a difference between light and darkness, one reveals truth the other hides it. There is a hunger to know the greater, but until the mind can comprehendible, it then becomes their reality. Knowledge is power and ower is knowledge, some good, some bad, knowing then, we can choose by informed truth. We often make judgement calls by what is presented to us by others revelatory insiders' scoops, sometimes without having all the information necessary to assess what is real and what is not. Beyond what I know is not always important to know unless it's key to a life threatening or altering situation that could possibly have a reparatory or consequential affect forever. Beyond what I know.

7

You and I

You and I were never meant to be alone, isolated, separated, imprisoned, kept from one another, because we were never created for that purpose, reason, or destination. You and I together can work as the synergistic force of making quantum leaps, bring the impossible into the possible realm, therefore, bring a game change in the outcome of what will be and what won't be. The power of two is always greater than the power of one, multiplying twice the power needed to accomplish the goals at hand. You and I represent the unity of two united fronts to achieve the ultimate purpose, a means to an end. You and I, the beginning and end, the front and the back, the top and the bottom, side to side, from all angles. You and I are the total sum needed to complete our journey in life. You and I have become one during the process of inclusion, merging nation, migration, infusion, blending our unique blends of knowledge, wisdom and understanding, completing the cycle of revelation. You and I.

1st Quotes

1. First come first serve. Chaos is created when there is no order or respect for all individuals
2. Truth is the only option that will give an individual opportunity to change from believinga lie or being deceived.
3. Sometimes obtaining knowledge can be costly, but don't be afraid to pay the price for Revelation.
4. Don't be afraid to take chances, you just might find the courage to succeed.
5. Life is full of uncertainties, but until you move beyond your certainties you may never know what is certain.
6. Fear can only keep you where you are unless you're willing to say no to it and yes to faith.
7. Greatness is discovered, potential is possibility, revelation is key, power is limitless.
8. Freedom is never without cost.
9. People say the more money the more problems, but I say the more problems you have the more money you need.
10. As people move from struggles of mental health dysfunctionalities to move towards normality's, there is light at the end of the tunnel.
11. If you don't own it, it isn't yours.
12. The handwriting is on the wall just decipher it
13. If you fail it's because you didn't have all the answers to the solution.
14. Chance is an equal opportunist, nobody has more, nobody has less.
15. Look at failure as a lesson to success, then you will know both sides

9

2nd Quotes

16. How many times you will fail before you realize you're doing something wrong?
17. From one's own perception they're 100% right, but from another you may be 100%
18. Life is like the rising of the tide, it comes in and goes out, sometimes unpredictable.
19. Words of wisdom is the life experience of another, if one takes heed, it capitulates them a head of the line.
20. Remember the past and you won't repeat it in the future if you pay attention.
21. If you have strength to start you have the will to finish.
22. It's impossible to reproduce another's dream because dreams are birth from the inside not the outside in.
23. Time is as good as you put it to good use, or you just squared and wasted it.
24. You can never reach the then and there until you complete the here and now.
25. Without the process of time nothing ever comes to the full manifestation of being.
26. Without truth you can never verify a lie.
27. Time will work for you and time will work against, you if you don't have the knowledge of the appropriate application.

28. Life will give you what you give it, if you give very little then you can only expect very little, but if you give very much then life should return the exact favor.
29. Life is like a seed, is like a seed being sown in the ground of life. It will live or die according to the amount of nurturing you give it.
30. As wind blows the eyes sometimes cannot see, but if you close your eyes, you can discern its direction by touch.

10

I Remember

I could never forget those unforgettable moments in time past when we knew each other. Our experience of deepness is deeper than deep. I've been exposed to truths nobody knows about other than me and you. Relationships are built upon the rudiment of trust. You trusted me with your prized possession. Your heart. You were willing to go the extra mile and allow me to explore your vulnerabilities, only given to those who possess a high security clearance of the highest nature. Your memories are imprinted upon the tablet of my heart that can never be erased from the depths of my consciousness. I remember the first time I laid eyes upon you, within a lifetime of reflection, I knew you were the one. I was aware that no other could ever replace the scent of your existence. I was complete. My heart was open to any and every challenge known to human involvement, to rectify for all the lost moments love was absent. I remember you were the revolution of my transformation, altering my cognitive comprehension of your gentle touch sending fire rushing up and down my spine, a mind-blowing exposure to my truth-ality, not my reality. I remember your beautiful smile like no other. It was yours that captured my craving, my thirst for more. Like the sun that shines so brightly in the morning time giving life to the lifeless your smile gave me not only life but hope too. I remember.

11

Don't Force It

Don't force it, it was never meant to be. Love was never meant to be forced upon another. The character of love is soft and gentle, tender, and sweet. Love is like a heavenly symphony, music to the heart. Love takes time to comply with the demands of those who have not yet experienced the touch of a Guardian Angel. Love by nature is selfless and tireless like nuclear plant with endless supply of comfort to go around. Love recognizes love when it sees it, feels it, touches it, hears it. Many think because they were able to manipulate someone into a relationship that will last. Be it far from the truth. It won't last at all. There's a difference between genuine love and Lust. Lust is an infatuation with the externals, but not the internals of the heart. Love is the internal workings of the soul that liberates one to freely give as well freely to receive. Love is a freewill agent seeking to express itself in the highest manner possible. Don't force it, it won't bend to the oppression of a slave master. Love is born in the wild and cannot be tamed by harsh treatments or confinement of any containment. The power that loves possesses is beyond any knowledge known to the human psyche. Love knows how to apply what is needed at the right time, the right place, with the right person. Love is an expert on its when's and when not. If you want love to grow, give it time. Don't pressure it, don't press it, don't push it, don't it hit, don't hurt it. And in time if tis meant to be, it will be. Don't force it.

12

This Latina

This Latina she was from a culture of many beautiful colors, of bright and florescent tints in nature.

Like the Sun, so warm, and light, she possessed beautiful insight into life, and the mysteries it carried. She was like no other I've ever encountered on the magnitude of magnificently, amazing.

Her eyes were like the café in coffee beans, a beautiful dark milk chocolate. She possessed the eyes of a seer with peripheral vision to bring tomorrow into the present, holding the future in the palms of her hands. As she walked before me my eyes glazed over with hope after beholding her bananas brown hues of mixed unconditional love. This Latina spoke life to the dead, and resurrected the hopes and dreams of those who lost confidence in their ability to believe once again. When she spoke, I saw truth through her spoken words of eternal life. Her butter milk reflection drew my attention to details as if she had already traveled into time past and understood all things. A gift from God to transform lives forever. This Latina.

13

In the Eyes Of

In the eyes of believing in love, one must be willing to go to the ends of the earth to prove its validation of realness. Seeing is believing, without works trust is nonexistence without proof of sincerity. In the eyes of love there is a need to showcase the attributes of giving and not looking for anything in return. I a deadening suspicion when people say I love without realizing the cost of not just talking about it but showing actions. In the eyes of love there's a variety of categories of specific types of love. Not all fit one the same condition or need. When engaging in a relationship develops into a deeper level of intimacy. Love takes time to grow into a full-blown romance that will stand the test of time. The roots of love grow deep, that's why it's important to know what you want and what you're willing to settle for. So many people get into relationships and tolerate all the nonsense of putting up with stuff they know they don't want to deal with. Love recognizes when fake love tries to perpetrate as genuine in an environment that requires pure truth and happiness only. In the eyes of love, it's willing give to the point of no return until that love turns into torment. For there is no torment in real love. In the eyes of love.

14

Revolutionary

Baby your love is revolutionary. It's radical about its pursuit of a deeper introspective of diving into the deeper than deep oceans of swimming without restrictions or restraints. Love at times is a wild emotion that wants to rule the world and have its cake and ice cream too. Love evolves with time as it grows with wisdom and understanding, as it transitions into a place of revolutionizing phase of moving beyond fear to capture the real essences of loving someone that is without measures. Since time began, there's been the grime syndrome association with pure a unadulterated rhapsody in its highest form of giving and receiving without cost. For so long people thought they could manipulate love by adding directives to this free game. Love will sometimes seem to be rebellious and defy all the protocols attached to its name. Love can never be contained in a limited sense in that it's the ultimate power of a changed heart. Revolutionary.

15

Reflection

Looking back in retrospect there were an occasion to regain what I lost in the mist of transitioning from some possible losses to redemption. As I reflected upon those moments, I saw the line of demarcation, a place of no return. The cost was more than I wanted to pay for the sacrifice I would soon discover it was not worth it the price I choice give in exchange for the pain. The pain has taught me that when making the wrong choices disappointment is ineradicable due to cause and effect. Reflection is the mirror which maintains decisions one wish they could undue but is sealed. Life is filled with regrets of missed opportunities of wishing I could undo the undoable. My introspection of what could have been sometime make me cringe at thought of the cost I've incurred over time. Time is a friend to no one. It doesn't always give you a second chance after the expiration dates. But one must learn from their own heartaches and mistakes because history has propensity to repeat itself if not carefully watched. Reflection.

16

Like Chocolate

Her eyes were like chocolate dipped in honey sprinkled with pure sugar. The sun won't shine in the morning time until she calls me by name. The moon won't glow in the evening time until she said so She was my addiction morning, noon, and night nothing ever went right. She had a hold on my soul like a Puppet Master in full control. Her eyes pierced the very core of my being leading me at her discretion. The power she wields with the look in her eyes was hypnotizing, mesmerizing. Like chocolate when the craving begins, she was my best friend. One look from those chocolate eyes of inventiveness was all I need to make it another day in this life. She was my chocolate conversation use your imagination, chocolate poured into milk and stirred up in cup sipped with a straw, by far she is the greatest of them all. Like chocolate.

Bittersweet

I often wondered how she could be **bitter** and sweet at the same time, kind of blow my mind trying to comprehend this enigma. As time unwind from the past to the present, I could see the many levels of degrees of difficulty from past life experiences. Life will be the greatest teaching one could gleam from if one would pay attention to all the small details. **Bitterness** comes from different outlooks on life and the interaction of participations of accepting the status quo of taking anything beneath their level of expectation. Oh, but the sweet is sometimes buried under the volcanic eruption of disappointments and failures due to un-insightful truth and liberties not incarcerated in the heart. Life can be a moment of topsy turvy if you're perception is scurrying for reality in a realistic manner if not careful could shatter one's dream. Being **bittersweet** is like sweet and sour, two conflicting tastes in the same spoon full of favor, but they seemed to go hand in hand, can't have one without the other. **Bitter**sweet

18

Silent Killer

Lo and behold, there's a silent killer lurking in the hearts of humanity. This silent killer kills every day, one by one and it's called love. It's not because there's too much love, but a lack of it. There's a power in love that can't be found anywhere in the universe accept through the conduit channeling. through the heart. The manifestation of this dis-ease is the epidemic of unfulfilled desire of connection with the other self. We long to be whole and complete, but never without the absences of love. There's been forms of what we call love, but it didn't fit the description or discipline. Some say it's called lust, but lust is simply a counterfeit perpetration of the real deal. Lust pretends to be real in nature, but in essence fake love is one of the deceitful culprits lurking in relationships. Love can't be given out a broken and unhealed heart. People want to be loved for the most part, but truly haven't recovered from the previous relation of disappointment and pain. Hurt people hurt people! The silent killer is loosed and recking havoc on potentially good relationships. Don't become a victim of the silent killer syndrome. Guard your relationships with all diligent. Silent killer

19

Beyond Recognition

Like a fairytale she was beyond recognition, but it was my mission to reveal truth that would set her loose from self-annihilation. I saw the inflation of a death sentence invoked by poor supervision of self-introspection and revelation. I thought I knew who she was until she began to spit venomous slang language I couldn't comprehend, her semantical conversation that made no common sense, but the situation became more intense as sand falling through an hourglass. And as time began to tic toc like time seeping into eternity, it appeared like I was gaining no ground to rebound a soul from its life right before me. But I was hopeful I could decipher her broken conversation to elevate her spirit from the abyss of total darkness. But there's light at the end of the tunnel. Truth be told all things are possible to them who believe in the impossible. There's a strength within the human psyche that is beyond their greatest potential and hold on to destiny. As I continue to reach into the depths of her soul seeking solace of peace of mind for this kind. Even though the battle rages I will fight to find an answer to this situation. Beyond recognition.

20

Time!

Time is disappearing as though it's seeping into eternity. With what time we have left, we must muse it as if it was a commodity of an investment that day shall return dividends or suffer a great loss. In life we've been allotted a certain amount of space to create to waste our gifts and talents. We must choose individually what will be or not be. Time gives us plenty of opportunities to investigate the best possible methods for gaining information key to our reformation or stagnation of growth. If one isn't motivated with the enlightenment of truth, then ignorance will heed the call to render its full support to those who are carless and unconscious of the ramifications of doing nothing. With time we can build, transform, erect places, things leaving a legacy that noteworthy of praise. What shall time testify of when we come to the last moments before it expires. Will time praise us for being good stewards or reprimand us for wasting the gold standard of life? Time!

21

Created in Love

I remembered while in the created state of my formation, I felt the hands of love presence. I've always existed outside of time, but at my appointed moment I would appear through the mandate of the Creator. As I watched His hands. I saw myself being sculpted like a Rembrandt, because of the power of love and life. As my being came into being, I was overwhelmed with a sense of peace while Angels assigned to me kept a watchful eye over my every move so that no harm would enter my abode, my secret place. Looking back in retrospect, I now realize I was fearfully made. I bear the DNA of my FATHER's blueprint with power and truth, second to none classified as perfected in His eyes. Nothing greater than the approval of being given life beyond the imagination. My ordination was ordained by the One who possesses all power. At His spoken word I appeared out of nothing into something. The full manifestation of the unseen into the seen. I was created in love.

22

Her Other Self

She can't seem to understand why life is so hard sometimes, as if her mind goes from one place to another trying to escape her other self, others can't understand her feelings and emotions, sometimes like a rollercoaster, but it was the words of others that caused her to lose her beautiful self, and still, there's no escape until she accepts her beautiful self, life isn't been easy, because of her ways of finding liberty just to be herself, her gentle soul begins to glow when she all alone, no pressure to be what others want to see, because her beautiful is not always in the eyes of the beholder, but the one who exhibits real life genuine passion for others, she's a trusted friend, loyal to them that understands her ways of being scars sometimes hide the inter beauty of dreams waiting to be revealed as she soars of like a eagle in the sky as it glides so freely without the help of others, she must see her others self as being special without second guessing her beautiful worth. Her other self.

23

Hidden In

Hidden in the crevices of time cloaked in incognito moments of concealment, I've always existed, but nobody exhibited the revelational endowment to discern my whereabout transitioned from eternity into time for temporary moments of reflection. Hidden in manifesto of being predestined to manifest the greatness within. Hidden in the annals of time the creative power was released while the architectural blueprint was being etched by pure hands. Time has not ceased to reveal the consecration of standard, being phenomenally enhanced by the divine will of the Creator. We're endowed with supernatural altitudes of soaring beyond the starts, traveling at the speed inception going pass the norm to the supernatural norm. Nothing is impossible to one who can grasp the concepts believing in the unbelievable. Hidden in.

24

If Walls Could Talk

If walls could talk, they would expose some of the most heinous crimes ever committed against humanity. The walls would give an eyewitness account of what transpired, when, what, where, why and who. The handwriting on the walls would begin to transcribe detailed information of the actual events by second, minutes, hours, days, weeks, years to reveal the whole truth, nothing but the truth. The walls would represent the Judge, jury, prosecutor, and defense all in one. The walls would etch in writing and drawing, not only telling the story in word form, but picture type markings also. The walls' voice would speak up for the victims and explain all gory facts that day. The walls would advocate for justice for the innocent victims of violence. The walls would identify the perpetrator and show in detail the events leading up to expiration of loss of life, property, vandalism, bodily harm, and intimidation to silence the voice of defenseless. If walls could talk there would be no cold cases, unsolved murders, no hidden secrets and nowhere for the lawless to hide. If walls could talk the innocent locked up for years due a flawed system, held evidence, a candidate running for office, falsifying information, tampering with evidence would be set free without second guessing the truth. Truth has a way of correcting lies, perjury, mishandling of sensitive information. If walls could talk, we would see a reverse situation of those in high position would replace a lot of those they sent to jail. It would be an enigma of life and death of things could change dramatically. There would equity instead of equality because of one level playing ground, not just in words but application of principles. No more ability to manipulate and control the scenario. No more puppet master shenanigan behind the scenes. If walls could talk and there were no exceptions to the rules, then the walls would no longer have to talk. If walls could talk.

25

Crossroad

I'm at a crossroad and not sure where to go from here. I made a decision I thought would improve my situation, but it turned out that things didn't go as I perceived. Now I'm trying to assess what went wrong. The question is, did it turn out for my good or that things didn't go my way or is there a better way. Sometimes you will never know unless you're willing to take some calculated risk. The blind will never learn how to walk unless he is trained to hear certain words and sounds to help him to walk without the assistance of a another. I don't always have the right answers or see the solutions to my pressing issues. When I come to a crossroad, I begin seeking counsel to find my way to the promised land. But when the outcome I'm seeking comes to naught, I questioned the decision I've made. Doubt tries to fill my mind with should have waited or did something different. One will never know until they're willing to make mistakes at the cost of success or failure. There will be many crossroads to travel to many mountains to climb, many valleys to tread and many rivers to swim in is part of life's journey. Crossroad.

26

Be Happy

One must learn to be happy for themselves. Far too long we try to please others because it's culturally politically correct. Albeit it is the truth. Other's truth is not always your truth. We just ago alone just to get along, and that's we're so miserable, misery loves company. We must learn what makes us happy not according to others might perceive too customary. Breaking family, community, or cultural norms isn't always easy as some might think. It takes work to get over the fears of others because we have allowed it to become our fears too. It takes two to tango not three, four or five. One must learn to set boundaries when involving others in other relationships making decisions. One should not look for others to make them happy; you should already be happy when you meet that special someone. It's too much pressure trying to create the perfect person. As we know nobody is perfect, but there's someone who will complement you, your alter ego some might say. It doesn't take much to be happy, it's a choice. Be happy.

27

Living Without Regret

As I look back in time so many mistakes were made that changed my destiny I sometimes wish I could go back in time and change My mind but it is what it is If I could of would of should of but that was back then I was so young and did not understand life's whole plan now that I'm a man I see things so much clearer My only problem was that I could see I needed a hero I believe in and that could've show me the way for a better day if I had known the tricks and trades of life I wouldn't have to fight so hard just to stay above water at times life is situational Like being on a rocky boat floating adrift lost so much time by saying what if no more time to lose as the clock tic toc, living without regret is where it's at living and learning from the past can be a lesson learnt and bought by the school of hard knots I must change my mind or will be locked in the past chasing a make believe that was never conceived My soul bleeds out its life into the what ifs as I drift down the sea of wondering thoughts moving at the speed of life looking back I got tricked in believing I couldn't make it But faith would dispel all the lies now I know it wasn't for nothing, but life has taught me. To learn from the past and to cherish the present and live the future without regret. Living without regret.

28

The Touch

I remember that moment when she gently embraced the palm of my hand. It was an unexpected act of consensual acceptance of her invitation to stand in solidarity. In that space of time, I read the language of the palm of her hand sending messages of hope and assurance. I felt the unification of her commitment to build together a sworn oath that would last forever. At that moment when our souls collided, our eyes began to glow with burning fires which turned into nova's of exploding visions which merged as one. The touch is a unique occurrence that only happens once in a lifetime. We were amazed as our hearts gazed over with a translucent coding of pure love and affection the protection of our covenant allowing some to see the manifestation, but we only knew the depth of deep intimacy. We both experienced the indelibly marking of our hearts being tattooed together while we both possessed half and half of the symbols to verify our destiny. The touch.

Coffee

Like coffee she has become my addiction ever since I can remember. I long for her in the morning time when I arise from my nighttime slumber. I never go a day without a taste of her invigorating, motivational inspiration. The smell of her brewing connects me with life and love to pass the time of day. Coffee is the first sip of the morning causing my atmosphere to dip into a world unknown to others, but I, myself. I love her because she's a vital part of my daily routine as I seek her out from various places. I often found her at home on the cabinet sitting there just waiting for my arrival to participate in the process preparation. Then other times I seek her through neighbor gas station grocery outlets, just standing there idly to be purchased by the one who her the most. My love for coffee has become a way of life, can't live without the power change that she makes in my everyday way of life. Coffee.

Pink Infidelity

She was soft and tender like smooth baby oil, this I remember on a day in September. She was like no other I've ever engaged with. I was caught up in the heavens because she was heavenly. Her words flowed like pink haze smoke that gazed my peripheral vision, oh did I mention that she laced my heart with conviction for a commitment of a lifetime of giving and receiving the full benefits of unconditional love. I caught pink eye due to my vision being burred from her glorious present, so did my heart imagine. Pink is a soft and tender reflection of vulnerability of being easily moved without much persuasion. The color pink has no loyalty to any, but to the one with the most convincing conversation. Pink infidelity.

What If?

What if I'm wrong about what I really believe to be real, wasn't real? I would have wasted a lifetime believing in a misnomer, fallacy or was it just a make believes convinced of the evidence not proven to seal the deal. Who's telling the whole truth or whose telling lies nothing but lies disguised as gospel, and not the gossip. There's a thin line between them both, who can know but the bearer of both. One can become self-deceived after chasing false-ailty and refusing to change the true narrative of the whole story. What if on one's death bed after hearing the truth and can't distinguish one reality from other, what would be the odds of that individual losing the bet or gambling the price of his soul? So, we take chances everyday betting that we're right until the truth comes forth and validate our conviction? What if

32

Beyond My Limits

Beyond My limitations There's a world of great potentially, just waiting to be had by those who are willing to move beyond their limitations. Greatness can be intimidating to those who never tried to lay hold upon its power. Greatness is waiting for the one who would stare it in the face and say, 'Bow your knees to me". To apprehend liberation to the road of freedom comes with a price that must be paid in full. One must press past the point of giving up and giving in. One must be able to see themselves out of the box, the borders of incarceration. If I must die trying by any means necessary to cross the lines of impossibility. One vision must be greater than their resistance greatness. In seeing one's own power will fuel their drive to fight for victory. No matter how many times they fail, they'll accept the status quo. Beyond my limitations is limitless opportunities to break every barrier to the apex of success. Beyond my limitations.

Vanilla Jones

My Vanilla Jones was of foreign decent, but she had a way of arousing my humanity not leaving my curiosity in check, only to free my folly from restriction of expression, becoming catalysis unto my unlearnt knowledge of seeking her out with intent of full-blown liberty. I had the green light to see all that was hidden from the naked eyes. The hunger deep within the circle of my dwellings grew with intense fervent craving needing the addiction of her presence within touching reach, I could peel the layers of truth I needed to move forward with full authenticity. Vanilla Jones was an enigma of the sweetest kind blowen minds, taking her time to gently killing me with her flavor, can't get rid of the addictions of her tender conversion, blowing my weakened conscious with sweet time. Vanilla Jones got me jonesing for more and more. Vanilla Jones.

34

How Did I?

How did I ever let you get away when I had you in the palm of my hands? You were mines. They said 9/10 is full possession by law. Your heart and love were for the taking, but I never fully took what you were offering. A lifetime of love. As I look back in retrospect, I wasn't able to close the deal on love. Ever since our last conversation, I've been having this" Uno a Uno" *talk with myself about how I allowed* someone else to steal the greatest treasure one could have ever had, the opportunity to keep. There's no answer. This question hasn't brought forth any comfort to the loss I've incurred, so long ago. My mind replays the moments I was letting you go with my words, but my heart was solidified with a covenant that none could ever break. Not in this lifetime nor the life to come. Now that I've chosen obligation over love, my heart has felt the struggles of forgiving me for committing treason against my soul. It was those touches of revelation that infected my reality with hunger. My thirst has ceased to be squelched since I've lost the right to drink from your free wells of liberty. We sometimes make decisions not fully understanding the whole impact of losing something so precious and dear. The lesson learned is I will never again lose the right to love when I have been given the blessings to walk into unconditional, transparent, passionate love. I've tasted heaven's gift for a space of time. And ever since those moments of illuminatory insight, I've not been the same. My exposure to true authentic butterflies has left me longing for the thrill of having someone who loves me and I them. How did I.

35

We Dipped

We dipped our souls in scented pleasure while musing about the texture of foreplay. Our feelings were laced with passion beyond imagination. Touches of grandiose displays played with our emotions while we searched playground loving. We jumped into the deep without fear of restrictions, without limitations. We gave each full permission to explore the depths of our endless souls seeking forever. We traveled to the end of the universal without passports or identification to go beyond expectations. We dipped our souls in a pot of liquid gold seeking to go deeper into complex places trying to find traces of our beginnings, fading into dreams of unmentionable. completability seeking freedom from each other. Feeling a plethora of dimensional, sentiment touch of relief from loneliness. We dipped ourselves repeatedly to experience the addictions of not being able to live without each other. We dipped.

36

I Beheld

I beheld your essence while gazing upon the reflection of your beauty. At times, I was lost for words, searching for an explanation of your magnificence. It must be spoken in several languages of words, touch, and the language of sign language of unspoken communication. I want to hold your silhouette while we dance slowly, as if we had forever and ever. The scent of your passion captured my vision of hope, as I entered your atmospheric dwelling where love is free to roam without restriction. I beheld your glory coming down from heaven escorted by supernatural beings draped in wonderful colors of mystery. Your hands are scented with lavender oils imported from the wilderness of freedom unrefined but purified with your approval. I held something beautiful that is almost unexplainable. As looked into your eyes I saw a passion beyond recognition. You are like no other I have ever known in this lifetime or the life to come. A moment of your time would be like spending eternal in the arms of unconditional acceptance. When I touched the palms of your hands, I felt the explosive powers of exhilaration flowing through my being like uncontrolled energy of a super nova, exploding right before our eyes. Life has not been the same since I have been exposed to the appearance of your presences. You are a wonderful remarkable sight, let not the moments of chance escape your ability to give and receive pure passion. I beheld.

37

Stop Falsifying

Girl, keep it real. I have seen so many sides of your alter-ego like watching a movie sequel of confusion or am I missing something? I know you multiple streams of emotions, kind like being on a rollercoaster with ups and downs and all around, tell me what you really want. Sometimes it is hard to read what you are saying because you go back and forward with this and that with all that fax of miscommunication. Be open and honest don't beat around the bush, is yes, or no? Stop falsifying those encrypted messages I cannot decipher for the life of me. Can't you just be a little like me, a little more logical? Speak a language you and I can together speak without crazy interpretation of unspoken clues. I know you mean well and that fine and dandy. It is not too late for us to get back on the right track and work this thing out before I jump ship and go AWOL (absent without out leave). Truth is the transparency of every relationship. No hidden agendas. No misinformation. No deception. No trauma. Stop falsifying.

38

Kit Cat Scratch Itch

Kit cat scratch itch—as she set in the chair, I was aware that she slowly began to scratch because there was a cat in the chair next to her, she said I'm allergic to cats and sometime they make me itch and go meow, and I said to myself she got the "kit cat scratch itch" what a trip and as we continue to sit in the meeting. I wonder if she was going to break out into hives, but I could tell that she was ready to yell, but she stayed cool, calm, and collect because she didn't want us to see her run out of the house with that kit cat rash, you know that's bad. But nothing happened and all was well. It's a dangerous thing to have an allergic reaction to something that makes you swell. I just want you to know that if you know someone with kit cat scratch itch to tell someone when they start to itch, not everyone wants to see them pitch a fit because you got the kit cat scratch itch. So be aware of the signs of swelling, inching and sometimes meowing, these are the symptoms of kit cat scratch itch.

I Wish

I wish you well on your journey to find what you are looking for. I can see you have been discontented with your present relationship, and nothing seems to appease your appetite for more. It seems like enough is never enough. I wish you well with finding the perfect person for you. Perfect is only in the eyes of the perfectionist. Your expectations run over into fantasy. Being imperfect is a blessing in disguise. They say, "Iron sharpens iron". We can never grow beyond our good times when there is no conflict. Sometimes trouble brings out the worst and the best in us. I wish that you can find closure in your search for what you perceive to be the right one. Sometimes grass isn't always greener on the others side. For some reason will assume that what we have is the worst relationship in the world while looking at others who are happy. Not knowing what it took to make the relations what it is. People nowadays do not know what to put in the work it takes to make a strong relationship stronger. Once we get pass the genie in the bottle mentality and deal with reality then we can truly grow out knowing not just wanting. Sure, we all would like a person that we never have any issues with, but that is not realistic being that everybody brings some type of baggage into the relationship. We should make the most of what little time we have in life. Many say life is too short to focus on petty stuff. We should not spend more time trying to fix the relationship instead of enjoying what you have been given temporarily. I wish.

40

Better Than

It could have been a lot worse than I thought. I have grown to appreciate what I have, seeing that my situation is rather good compared to others. I have no reason whatsoever to complain about how terrible things are after seeing how bad other people's relationships are in comparison to mine. I believe I have been blessed with the best. It's all about perception and how you look and think from a negative situation or from a grateful position. My life is better than I could have ever imagined. I am so happy that I got a reality check from a non-biased point of view that turned my life around. Because of your teachings, I see life in a whole different light. No longer I am I blinded to the truth, but free to exercise liberty. Better than.

Dream

I had dreams of your Carmelitic layered sweet, scented aroma flowing through my awareness of your presence. I was intoxicated with the history of your beginning and ending. My taste buds were aroused every time you came into the circle of my living spaces. My hunger was increased by the incessantly and could not be appeased until you said please. The tenderness of the vanilla-soaked mocha covering was more than enough for a lifetime or two. Let brush your black silk hair woven by angels while sleeping the sleep of love. My thirst can never be quenched just by several sips of craving for you from your well of endless pleasures. I want to squeeze you gently while whispering secrets of your hopes and dreams. Dreams of you are visions of hope and intrigue of how blessed to have as mines and when I touched the palm of your hand there was an awakening from the unknown to the known. I feel the vibration of your heart from a distance, discerning your every need and want. Oh, how I want you! My addiction grows stronger and stronger every day you are gone from my presence. Dream.

I Want To

I want to kiss your candy yam lips while squeezing your tender pillow soft body in my arms. I thirst for your liquid love from your wells of endless waters of life. I want to gaze into the mirrors of your soul to provide you with a menu of love. I want to hold you but for a moment of time before eternity starts and never unwind. Every time I see you, I want to possess the flow your emotions right into my hands where you will feel safe and secure. I want to dance the night away until the break of dawn while the birds chirping songs of joy as though we're at a concert. I want to smell the morning dew of your body fragrance to start my day. Oh, how I feel the vibrations of your conversation when you whisper softly after being caressed all night long. Your sweet melodies comfort my world day and night. I crave the very thought of you lying right by my side knowing that you are safe. I want to.

43

Stained

My memory seems to be stained with past failures of not doing the right thing. My convictions have labeled me as being guilty without a judge and jury. I am imprisoned by weaken conscious of not doing the right thing when it was the right time. I can't go back in time and undo the undone situation that chases me down life's path. I must learn to control my thoughts, least I become a victim of my own mistaken understood analysis. Being stain is like a mark you can't erase with chemicals or stain removers. The memory has had a way of bringing balance to unbalanced events in your life. I must learn the art of forgiveness to maintain my own sanity. Stains are the mistakes we made without all the knowledge to make an informed decision. At time we wish we could turn back the hands of time and reverse the infractions made uninformedly. Stains sometimes can leave nasty marks upon a perfectly well intended situation that didn't go the way you planned. So much for that! Life is the school of higher learning, and we do not always learn the lesson before us. But at times we crash like a crash dummy. Everybody has in their lifetime got a stain or two. It is part of the process of living and learning. Stained.

I Bet

I bet you're still stuck on stupid, doing the same old thing trying to get different results. You just need to take a chill pill and go somewhere and sit down and stop clowning around. How many times do you need to bump your head before you really get it. They say "A hard head makes a soft behind" if you know what I mean. I bet if you don't change your ways you will end up where you started, nowhere. It's not that difficult to make changes, you just need a made-up mind. You see, life will give you what you give it. Kind of like a sowing and reaping philosophy if you know what I mean. Well maybe not. Things haven't changed all this time I don't know if it ever will the rate you're going. I bet when it is all said and done you will end up in the same old place. I bet.

45

Antithesis

She was like an antithesis of the night and day. Sun and Moon. Water and fire. Warm and cold. Love and hate. In and out. Sunshine and rain. Polarization opposing opinions of beliefs can't seem to agree on the same thing and nothing remains the same. Like two spectrums of intertwining philosophies that speak from a distance. To go against the beliefs of another can only create confusion and frustration in my estimation. Sounds kind of crazy! It goes against the juxtaposition belief of trying to compare two side by side making it exceedingly difficult to come to the place of probability or non-probability. Her ways had to be deciphered by learning the ways of how she functioned on a normal and abnormal level. The question is she living a double life or a double personality. Who's knows! Antithesis.

46

Cold Winters

I've lived through myriads of life winters weathers; it was a conflict of changing weather or relationships. The only thing they say in life that is consistent is change, and for some reason you never get used to it. Not always sure why, but the lessons in life are taught, but you can bet it won't let you forget. Frigid winter can remind us how painful memories can be. Something we forget but it seems like past events are like great painting on the ceiling of our minds, etched there forever. Life also brings summertime seasons into one's life as well. Summer times season are those which seem to flow without any restriction or barriers, kind of like happy times of being on a honeymoon. Cold winter are season which seems like everything had dies and there seems to be no life after death. But would not all true. Cold winters start the process of living and learning during the good times as well as the bad. Cold winters.

Stains

Stains are indelible marks of distinctions left from prior events of influential transaction of good, and bad in our thought process. In life we would like everything to be perfect, but life has a way of bringing a balance of equal portions justified ability. Events of time past distance past change the fortitudes of our decision-making process. Stains are a daily reminder that you're stuck with me regardless of how I feel. At time we can suppress difficult situations we long to forget, but somehow the unconscious memory bank sends signals to remind us that I'm still here" remember me". We often try different apparatus to deflect painful reminders of so long ago. We must face out past with courage and intend if we're ever to heal from crippling reflection of yesterday's disappointments. It is never too late to recover from disappointment if we make the choice, we want something new. Stains.

48

Moment

For a moment in time, I felt this emotion called love. Though I've never understood it before that space of reflection I now know. When I said I loved her eyes she smiled and responded back by saying I love you too. I felt this one to connect for the first time. It was a wow moment. Everything I said was yes, I feel the same way too. We were in total alignment, perfect synchronization, real attachment, it was heaven sent. And when she reciprocated the spoken revelation, I know she was mines, and I was her true love. Love has the strongest foundation of success when two people prefer one over the other. Always giving each other priority. It's been said that it's better to give than to receive. There's a true joy in putting the ones you love first. For a moment I understood her needs and wants from her facial expressions. She was elated and overjoyed just being in my presence. Something wonderful happened as we communicated our love language for one another. For a moment.

49

Somethings

Somethings are not to be. Now I see all this time I was chasing someone who was not meant to be. I now realize it was never mines. I just toyed with the thought of how wonderful it would have been not having counted the cost. Somethings are not for everyone, just for someone in particular. How do we waste so much time pursuing false dreams and unrealistic fantasies that only lead to misery. Freedom is the art of recognizing that it may seem that it's compatible, but in retrospect it would not have made you as happy as you thought. I'm so glad the answers to some prayers have been "No". Sometimes no can save you from years of disappointments and disillusionment. Looks can sometimes be deceiving and misleading. It takes more than just being beautiful on the outside, but the inside too. Sometimes people are filled with regret because they thought that he or she was it. If only they slowed down the process of jumping headlong into the relationship without doing their due diligence. Without these three things surely, there will be a lot of confusion in the growth of potential good relationships: knowledge-information, understanding facts and wisdom-application. As time transpires in relationships it begins to reveal the weakness and strength of that relationship giving one insight on how to navigate the relationship without falling into the pitfalls of despair. Somethings.

50

No Smoke

Why do some people think that they won't some smoke? It's kind crazy when you have the right of way and people don't comply with the rules of the street signs. Stop means to stop at the stop sign, but some people disregard safety rules. They appear to be mad as hell and get an attitude because you had the right of way of driving first when they violated the law. What nerves! She had the gall to get upset about being in a hurry and not wanting to wait her turn. She acted like she wanted to throw some "knuckle sandwiches" by raising her fist in displeasure. I thought to myself "she doesn't want no smoke". But in her mind, she was blinded by her rage that I would dare make her wait. But she had it twisted because she misinterpreted as a sign of weakness, but it was a display of meekness. Never underestimate the other person regardless of their looks. Never judge a book by the book cover. It just might be more than you bargained for. No smoke.

51

Cold Piece

She was a cold piece like nothing I've ever seen, somewhat like a bad dream, scheming and deceiving, like a gold digger with fool's gold dust fever thinking she a diva, a she believer. She was convinced that what she is what she was meant to be. She is cold as ice with a bit like a sharp knife she will cut you and spit you out like dreadful day. You better learn how to pray. She cold like cold stone ice cream without a dream because she isn't sweet as honey and all she won't is your money. She is wild and a poisonous berry, nothing she does will make you happy. She became cold after being told she was worthless time after time again. She had a point to proof to those who use her love and good will for free, thinking that she was easy like taking candy from a baby. But time would reveal her truth for revenge. Never take a woman for granted you just might regret it. She can be hot as fire or cold as ice. It all depends how she is treated by the others. Cold piece.

52

Fleeting Memory

It was just a fleeting memory of yesterday's past thoughts. A Deja vu, it's like a replay of a reality played out before my eyes. Fleeting memories captured inklings of partial revelation where you almost got it but quite not. Fleeting memories are like searching for hidden treasures without full discovery. Fleeting are dream thoughts partially revealed in bits and pieces forever seeking the true meaning of what you perceived. Thoughts come and go. If you are not paying attention, you'll miss the whole interpretation. Fleeting memories carry both conscious and subconscious mind translating messages of deep interpersonal revealing's. Fleeting memories.

53

Finest Moment

This could have been your finest moment. All your life you've searched for that one true love. Due to your mishaps and mistreatment, you have caught a case of maybe it looks, sounds, and feels kind of shady. As I recalled, wasn't his Grady? With missed cues of the blues, you ain't been happy ever since you been fooled into thinking that narcissistic love was the favor of the hour of choice bur it only more chaos into your heart. You say you were looking for a hero, didn't they call him Leroy or was sweet Ricky they said he's kind tricky. This could have been your finest moment when I gazed into your honeycomb, almond shaped, multi-blended color changing eyes. Baby, I know how to flip your switch according to how I want your twitch, shake, rattle and roll, causing your eyes burn like flaming fires of sincere desire. This could have been your finest moment if you understood real love standing right before you. Finest moment.

?

They're so many? I have that's unexplained. Uncertainty blocks the mind from conceiving truth that gives eyes to its tangible reality. Like a blind man seeking to find his way from point A to point B seems to be a mystery until he completes his journey. Only occurs when the answers are hidden from plain view with no clues to give step by step directions. Could be the reflection of being lost without the cost of knowing as one should know. Like King Kong our problems seem to be bigger than life, almost unconquerable. But nothing in life that is too difficult or hard is beyond the reach of being overcome with persistence and fair. Life is full of unanswered? we've still trying to figure it out. I guess everyone needs some closure to what, when, where, why and how? Life has a way of giving us bits and pieces of the puzzle only to still leave us in limbo.

55

After Thought

Have you ever regretted a decision you made and wished you could go back in time and change? Have you ever been in a conversation and later wished not that you had time think about it and interject a different thought or ideal that would have been more in your favor? Some of the greatest conversations pieces came through my afterthought. I wished on many occasions I could return to a conversation I had from the past to prove my point. But it's too late. Time has moved into the future leaving behind has transpired from the past. At times wishing I was a time traveler. After thoughts always seem to have a greater insight than the present thought you thought about while you were thinking about at that moment in time. Sometimes our greatest revelations don't arrive until time has settled in the subconscious mind. After thoughts are just simply thoughts we thought about later after the conversation has ended. Afterthought.

56

Just Maybe

Just maybe it's not as bad as it looks. Sometimes we find ourselves in situations trying to figure out how did I get here? Life has a way of bringing you to a crossroads of uncertainty whereas you are now forced to make some difficult choices with or without your consent. Just maybe you created a situation where there is no other recourse but travel the road paved right before your eyes. Someone once said, "you're dammed if you do or dammed if you don't ", not a lot to choose from. There's always hope when things seem to be bleak and unassuming. Just maybe if we take more time with making important decisions and getting trusted counseling, just maybe it would turn out to be more in your favor. Nothing greater than life going your way. I know it sounds crazy, but just maybe it will work out. Just maybe.

57

Serial Lover

I'm just a serial lover. Can't help myself from loving people unconditionally. My heart has changed from hate to love. I find myself forgiving those who have done me so many injustices. Ever since I've been given a life sentence of love, I must return the favor now that I got me a savior. Serial lovers love regardless of the circumstances or situations. Forgiveness is not predicated upon how good or badly someone acts. Serial lovers go beyond the point of just love, but commitment, feelings got nothing to do with it. And you know this. Without serial lovers in this world, it would come to a screeching halt. Instead, it seems like at times we have more serial haters than lovers, but it would seem to be that it's the farthest from the truth. Serial lovers rarely get sick because love heals more than sickness causes one to reel from the ills of being poisoned from within, then again, we must choose our cup choice. Serial lover.

My Soul

I want you to hold my soul for moments of essential needs. I feel your presence when I reflect upon everything that you mean to me. I feel the power of your touch when you caress my mind upon your breast feeding me from the revelation of your beginnings. You are incredibly wonderful leaving a secret imprinted trail of mystery and intrigue graving more of what you possess. My soul longed for more than the natural but the supernatural. I can't seem to curve this insatiable appetite for all that you feed during your times of visitations. I'm like a prisoner trapped between your and my world. My hunger for the knowledge lies within the memory banks of your intuition of connecting the dots of real feelings. My soul longs to merge as one entity throughout eternity. Just you just me. My soul.

59

Sugar **Free**

Baby your love is sugar free of all artificial sweeteners. Your love is as pure as it comes. Like honey on the honeycomb, like sweet Sugar Cain, not processed with all the extra stuff to dilute it from its original intent. With one stir from those luscious fingers, I'll never have to buy anything else to make my coffee taste so delicious. Every time I embrace your sweet silhouette my sugar levels go sweet ecstasy. My heart starts to race like a high-performance racing car revving ready to go. Baby your sweet as candy yams cooked melted butter simmered slowly in crock pot over night. Sugar free.

60

Chances

Chances happen to us all, some rise, some fall. Sometimes opportunity comes disgusting as maybe, maybe not. If you recognize a moment of change you could possibly rearrange destiny. Perception is everything when it comes to moving into greatness or getting left behind to continue to grind the fine line. Check your mind to make sure that you implore your truth to prove to yourself that all things are possible to them that believe so don't be deceived. Opportunities comes and go, make sure you like the flow of how things are going, or you'll be coocoo for coco puffs. The ride could go against the grain leaving nothing but a little taste of shame, but don't worry or be in a hurry to get the end, it will have the same results sooner or later. There is 24 hours in a day, and everybody is allowed the same measure of time it all depends upon the mind that execute its own plan. Chances.

61

Until Forever

Time will one day become eternity. Time is simply moments locked in until it is released forever. Forever in a day let us make the most of the fleeting moments sometimes taken for granted. Life lessons are to live life, not allow life to live you. Until forever we must invest time as if it is golden. What you value the most you will give careful attention to as if you are experiencing your last moments of joy, happiness, and elation. The great spaces of time are those inklings of period of memories when we smile because all is well. Quiet atmospheric environments allow us to feel and know the magnitudes of our blessings. Until forever, until time is transferred into eternity, let you, let me, let us, let them take advantage of what is an opportunity of lifetime, the ability to give and receive by choosing to love and do no harm. Until forever.

Why?

Why must I feel this way I thought grace would be by my side when things Went array as if I Strayed From a place of safety Why have I caught a case of disappointments time After time nothing to Filled this rhyme but sadness and disgrace has replaced My joy with what if I feel like I've been stiffed with Ifs, buts and maybes trying to separate myself from this ain't me why must I Grieve by the grave sites of nights without PEACE Can't seem sleep at the hours of rest I've done did My best or is it test of My faith can't tell if the Well has run dry just Trying to survive another Night of unrest at best Where is grace I still face Endless rendezvous of the clock Tic Toking ring a ding ding No time for false themes and counterfeit dreams My eyes are red from the Dead sleepless night Up fighting with insomnia can't seem to find my Way to heaven's gate to evaporate and escape This nightmare does anyone care flared with fire of non participation, no revelation to state my case No power to erase this base though of whose fault is it don't dismiss this an occasional incident with Complications in my Estimation dealing high Inflation prices too to Apply for compensation why, why, why can't afford Another lie before I die Can a I get a break, but things continue to shake, rattle and roll before You know I 'll be selling solid gold hits Why, when, and where cannot stand all this nonsense ain't trying to complain Tire of playing this same old game. Why?

The Voice from The Womb

I hear a voice crying out from the womb long after the abduction of its life. The voice reverberated with echoes of disparity through the place it once aboded, wondering why they or them was evicted so abruptly. The previous residents once felt safe until they lost their legal rights to be. There was no verbal consensus to the act of the law of procreation being revoked by non-caring participants in a game of chance or Baby Russian Roulette. So often the voiceless one loses out to the majority vote. Being that they were always at the mercy of the joy seekers. It's dangerous for the newcomers who heard of the right to free speech or the first amendment. It's a difficult situation to be at the mercy of the merciless. The question is who will protect those who cannot protect themselves from the abuse and misuse of life invaders when it is no longer popular to be inconvenienced by a lack of protective measures before yielding oneself to procreation permission. The life was in the blood ,therefore, it spoke as an advocate for the party that was taken from the department of full development. The voice still speaks from the place from which blood was spilled.

Is It Real

Sometimes it seems hard to believe when life has taken a turn for the worst. It's been said if it's too good to be true it just might be valid statement. But not in every case. I guess many of us can identify with a few rough patches along the roads to finding something that's meaningful. Maybe the question may be what is you're looking for? Life is full of counterfeit relationships, more like knockoffs at a swap meeting. Everybody is trying to sale something that ain't quite genuine. Real relationships come with some baggage, hopefully, no more than you care to deal with. Bad relationships can leave a bad taste in your heart if you don't take measures to deal with all toxic episodes of being in a supportably elusive relationship. We must learn that relationships come with some measures of adjustment. If you have been hurt, betrayed, or disappointed, welcome to the club. But let one bad apple spoil it for everyone else. After having an encounter with the bad sides of dating, don't think that there's not possibly great good ones around the corner. If you don't succeed many times, you have tested the waters, find the courage to try again, you just might find what you're looking for. Is it real.

65

They Got the Hooch

They got the hooch cha mama bad, wearing them daisy dukes short with all that crack hanging out Anit doubt what kind of message they trying to send to the men and boy looking for a play toy. It's almost like they got the fever to show case all their goodies. Driven by greed and fame, wanting to hang out with the mentally insane gang. They seek wildlife, nightlife, and the fast and furious life only to end sooner than later. Moved by fast cars and the bling bling with fake dreams and all those other things. Groomed at a young age for the streets to meet the demands of those with evil deeds, feeding the greed. They got the hooch looking in all the wrong places for their needs to be met but catch a case of emptiness. The sale their souls for a little of nothing believing that struck gold only to turn out to be fool's gold. Life seems to be a vicious cycle of chasing false hope to help them when they get all dropped up because they got the hooch.

66

Sunshine

Like the sun shines so bright. Your illustrious illumination is simply a combination of revelatory information confiscated by my intellectual ability to decipher your inner workings of beauty. Your light sometimes blinds my mind to depths of your deepness. You're deeper than deep. My mind at times cannot comprehend your magnificence. All I can do is call you sunshine. You make me feel so light, so bright so tight because you got the right stuff baby. Every now and then you make feel alright. Sunshine continues to shine like the blind rage love in the heart of a mad man. Your sunshine is the epic center of living made worthwhile. Everybody loves the sunshine.

67

Transfusion

The life is in the blood. After losing so much blood I began to feel death trying to pull me to the other side. But I saw life at the end of the tunnel. Death was on one side beckoning unto me to join a group disappearing individuals passing from life to another. But I wasn't having it. The loss of one's blood can cause tiredness and dizziness at times almost losing consciousness. We sometimes give our sweat and blood to people and organizations that don't appreciate who you really are. Taking for granted your hard work and commitment. One must recognize their own very and self-worth and not demoralized when you're not picked as "puppet of the month ". Never let anyone have such control of your self-image that you can't function individually. Always needing a dose of their approval. Sometimes we just need a transfusion of people in our lives that will bring out the best in us and not the worst. Transfusion.

68

Just Say No!

I'm just tired of all he-hawing, going along to get along, and being a team player. Sometimes I felt pressured to put up with a lot of nonsense just to make other people happy. No is the answer I really want to say but it's not like team like behavior. I know am not the only one that feels gaged up with a group of people I could surely live without. No wouldn't be any love loss. Because our lively hood depends on how well we can maintain comradery or tolerate the distasteful demeanor of the worst kind. Navigating the dislikes of undesirable of ugly kind can a very daunting at best. On many occasions I wanted to scream out, no! No can be a very positive thing when dealing with people who only substructure and divide from your life. Like blood suckered, leeching off everything that lives within you. Just say no!

69

Living for A Memory

How often we're living for a memory. A thrill that could kill. Life will pass you right by if you're not paying attention. Time is the greatest commodity you will ever possess, be careful how you handle it. Like sand in the hourglass slowly sipping from one dimension to another. Once the movement stops so does the power to change. Living for the moment can only render fleeting moments of excitement that quickly dissipate. Like going on a roller-coaster ride once you reach the top and you drop to the bottom, it's over just that quick. Life should have meaning and purpose. For without it we only enjoy spaces and places. Living for the moment. reach the top and you drop to the bottom, it's over just that quick. Life should have meaning and purpose. For without it we only enjoy spaces and places. Living for the moment.

70

It Just Looks Bad

At times things look worse than they truly are. They say looks are deceiving if you're looking from the outside in. Sometimes you just can't tell what's what. I've had a myriad of second-guessing moments where I wondered what was really going on. And at times I've questioned my own faith. Trouble is temporary, but can seem a lifetime of waiting for change. Perception is in the heart of the perceived. To determine the outcome of a difficult situation you must beware of the ins and outs. Sometimes life just looks bad, but don't allow those spaces of unexpected surprises to break your dreams. When life becomes too much to bear make sure that you have a great support group that pulls you through the toughest of times. It just looks bad.

At times things look worse than they truly are. They say looks are deceiving if you're looking from the outside in. Sometimes you just can't tell what's what. I have had a myriad of second-guessing moments where I wondered what was really going on. And at times I have questioned my own faith. Trouble is temporary but can seem a lifetime of waiting for change. Perception is in the heart of the perceived. To determine the outcome of a tricky situation you must beware of the ins and outs. Sometimes life just looks bad, but don't allow those spaces of unexpected surprises to break your dreams. When life becomes too much to bear make sure that you have a great support group that pulls you through the toughest of times. It just looks bad.

71

Never Return

We can return to our formal state after entering past the line of no return. Once we cross that line of no trespassing we have willfully, consensually agreed to the terms of the rules, regulations or violation. It then becomes written in stone that all participants must abide by what is. Whether the terms render the good, bad or ugly. There's no changing the outcome of what must be. One must count of the count before engaging into any covenant that may render issues the down the road that may not be to your liking. Its too late to undo the intimate encounters once you have touched, tasted and handled that which you have pursed you can unlearn those memories that becomes a stain on your conscious. Something the heart can never forget. One must be sure when entering into any kind of contractual deal that will allow you to experience a lifetime of love or lifetime of pain. Once you said yes then you agreed to all the liability and assets that comes with that situation. Never return.

72

Deep Side of Love

How can one measure love see that it has no limitations, like a bottomless pit so love fits the Bill, to give one's life would be an example of total sacrifice, not withholding anything from the one who is so undeserving. What is this deep love that goes beyond forgiveness to liberate the guilty, vindicate the captive, to release you and me from misery, how can this be? No one could ever measure the boundaries of true deep love. Love is a power beyond our total revelation and sometimes our comprehension. Love has a deep side that causes us to flee from it so, therefore, many may never experience it due to the abuses situation they've encountered along this journey. What a shame! Deep side of love.

73

Ticking Time

It seems like time is ticking without purpose. As I sit pondering whether I should be here or somewhere else. Time is like a commodity; how will you invest it? Time must not be wasted by doing nothing, but something that is profitability. You can't get time back once it expires. Having a purpose and a plan to maximize your opportunities to make a difference. Time is the only gift of privilege of possessing for an abbreviated period of time. What you put in is what you get out of time. Time has compound benefits of giving you more than you given it. Many have squandered vast amount of time that can't be recovered. Like boiled water on top of a stove as it begins to vaporize into thin air no longer to exist as we know it. With every tick there a toc, so make the best of the time we possess while it is still called time. Like the beat of a heart with every tick brings us nearer to the end. Ticking time.

74

My Greatest

When I realized in an instance of that moment it was my greatest moment. There shall never be a greater awakening in the space of time when my epiphany became my revelation that you're the one. At that moment I took to heart that the love I've been searching for was here in the here and now. You represent everything and more I've been searching for. My travels to the promise land has come to an end. For that which I've prayed for is now mines. No blinded moments of maybes or this feels kind of crazy. The peace of my destiny has arrived. No more dreams for me for I can feel my redeemed one in my arms holding me tight and never letting go. My greatest moment was the moment I realized that I was destined to know and love would find it's way into my path of life. My greatest moment.

75

Somebody Else

While going through these tests and trials, I would rather be someone else until it's over. Nothing more difficult than being in the center of a storm. Life will bring many days of unexpected situations you would prefer not to deal with. I constantly ask myself the question, why? What's the purpose for these pressing problems? Far too often there appeared to be no relief in sight. Life would be perfect if I had a surrogate substitute to take my place while I rest on a bed of ease. I'm quite sure no one would apply for that position with the exception of money being involved. Some people would dare to spend a night in hell for the right price. There's a price for any and everything. Somebody else.

76

Green Cat Eyes

That's cat meows with those beautiful green eyes. As I gazed into those lush flush valleys of her peripheral vision I got the green light know that's right. There's something that makes my heart take notice of something wonderful. Green cat eyes are special in that fact that it takes two nations to create. A mixture of multiple shares blended diverse cultures handpicked to volunteer themselves to bring forth this wonder. When I behold one with green cat eyes it takes my perception to whole different level of comprehension. Blessed are those born with green cat eyes. May they live forever. Green cat eyes.

77

The Reward Outweigh the Risk

The rewards outweigh the risk, therefore, I'm willing to take the chance, In the game of life it's sometime all or nothing, and human instinct when it takes over it will find a reasonable way to do it, there's no logical reason for what has transpired human survival assumes command which seems to be irrational in nature whether lawful or unlawful. The rewards outweigh the risk when that which one seeks is unusually permanent and the risk is temporary. Due to the gains and loses the gains always carry a great motivation to pursue the greater good. There will be times when one begins to question their motives for the goals they set for themselves only to find a struggle of whether "I should or I should not". The doubt come from running into so many roadblocks only to ask if "Lady Luck" is on their side. At this point one must consider all things considering the best solution for the greatest outcome. The purpose for the drive to take the risk is the prize for which one is willing to sacrifice all for the supreme victory. To apprehend the reward, the risk will always seems greater, but the reward is the means to an end. Once you go through the process of getting what you have set your heart upon you realize that the reward outweighs the risk. The rewards out outweigh the risk.

78

Tomorrow

Tomorrow is never promise to anyone, we live with expectation that by the grace of GOD that we were spare another day. We must live today like it's no tomorrow. Tomorrow may never come again. We have been free from the downsides of life only to show gratitude for all GOD has entrusted us with. When opportunities present themselves, we must embrace it as if it's the last chance to enjoy the privilege of servicing such a great GOD. Let everyday be a blessing to others that they may enjoy the joys of knowing that every day is a gift and not to take it for granted. Tomorrow.

79

My Alkebulan

In the Garden of Eden where I first discovered you were the mother of all mankind. I fell deeply in love with your dark reflection of **Blackness**. I laid beside you in the flush push green fields of the mother land of comfort before time began. Your blood ran through the pipelines of my veins resurrecting the life I now know. Oh, how I love you with an eternal passion beyond one's comprehension. They concealed your true identity to steal the richness of your fertile grounds of endless resources, globally supporting the world from the breast milk of abundant supplies. Many have come and gone using the tree of life as a source of endless resource to all those who have stolen your hidden treasures of abundance. Many lives have been sacrificed all in the name of greed. My roots run deep within the fertile soils of your rich grounds. The blood of many cries from the harsh treatment you endured for centuries because you were ravished of your innocence by the hands of strangers. You seemed to have lost your identity, but I remember who you are my beloved. I shall always love you. My Alkebulan.

80

Samurai Love

No power greater than a Samurai love. She was pale by nature reflecting the white orchids lace with cherry blossom lips. Injustice is met with a sword righteousness and honor. The true love of a Samurai is to uphold the code of integrity in the highest form. A Samurai love is shown through his commitment of historical tradition and customs. The Katana is welded with precision and accuracy to avenge every wrong. Love only grows in an environment of truth and purity. Samurai love carries the sounds of a poetic vibration emanating from the souls of warriors heeding the call of loyalty. Samurai love.

81

Tombstone

Her empty heart was like a tombstone, nothing living. There was no sign that life had ever existed. A hollow cave of vibrating memories of what transpired some ages ago. Cobwebs and dust have taken up resident in the dance halls where joyful spoken words are no longer recited to revive love. In a place once filled with unspeakable passion, now lies doormat. How can one's heart go from life to death, from peace to confusion, softness to hardness? Life is filled with complicated situations that's difficult to understand. Tombstone.

82

The Light

You're the light of my life when darkness wants to have its way. My truth when deception wants to hide Your face. My hope when despair wants to cast You away. When confusion wants to dim my path You become my glorious light. Truth then becomes reverently real. Your touch of love surrounds me like a guarded treasure. Your presences encompass the whole of my existence, my purpose for being. Like a dream I only know in part because of your magnificence's it hard describe You in mere words. You're the revelation to my complications of trying to figure out how to love You in the purest form. There is none like You that ever existed. The light You posses is the power of life. My sole purpose for living in the light. The light.

83

One Away

There's a thin line between love and hate, life and death. Life's a gift so don't take it for granted, you just might wish one day you hadn't. I've had some close calls with the other side of this thing called life. It was a very dark situation. I've come to grips that we're one stroke, one heart attack, one breath away from being no more. Life just don't happen, for every action there is a reaction. As creators we sometimes create situations not conducive to happy ending. We must take evaluations about whether or not we can live with the imagination of our mind. Life is but a fleeting vapor of temporary existence as it appears for a moment of time only to disappear forever. Surely life has its upside and downs. We cannot control everything that comes into play, so we play the hand dealt to us. One away.

84

Long Journey from Home

All she can remember is being in this damp and dark hell. Getting sick from being shackled in this strange vessel that goes to who knows where. All she remembers is being captured in my home and dragged to the seashore of death. She has many memories of callous treatment from those with white ghost skin. I thought they were demons from another dominion. I saw the fire of hate in her eyes as if she was a hunted prey. It's been a long journey home from what she uses to know. She lost my native tongue. she was forces to speak to speak with a fork tongue like those who took her from her homeland. I have nightmarish dreams of being tortured by evil hands. she never knew a race of people could be so cruel. I remembered the death of those who didn't make it across the troubled waters but were cast over the side of the ship. The stench of death filled the ship while tracking of her unwillingness to go a diaspora. The Motherland cries because of the separation from the soil from which gave her life, no longer will she ever nurse from the breast which gave her hope but has lost all she has ever known to the darkness of her presence in a strange land. Long journey.

85

Her Touch

Her touch I've longed for. Just the thought of her caused my awareness of love to grow even stronger. I remembered her black licorice scent mixed with vanilla liquid, the power of her presence was before me. My heart pounded like the thunder of a raging storm. I thirst to drink from the wells of her bottomless living waters. I desired to be hand feed from the silhouette of her predestination of living life to the fullest. Her touch felt like purple velvet knitted by the hands of a created imagination of greatness. Her truth became my truth, her heart became my heart, we emerged as one. I rediscovered the power of loving through the strokes of passion. Touch has the power to heal a broken heart in spite of the depths of pain. I recognized the configuration of textured imprint upon the surface of truth. Her Touch.

86

Night Breeze

Oh, how the sun has scorched my melanated hue a little more. On the heat of the day, I worked without mercy insight. The master's only concerns are that he works me like a mule by using a whip to beat me when it looks like I am just being lazy. But he has no clue what it is to work until I am about to pass out. I work from sunup to sundown. Sometimes we would pray for death or an opportunity to escape even if it meant being publicly humiliated. The night breeze was a sign that we could finally rest from our master cruel forced labor. At night we would pray and sang songs in code about our freedoms and how we could escape without little chitlins. The night breeze was GOD given us a cool bath to heal our broken bodies from the torcher of the sun and from the lashes of the strap for which bore the scares to remind us to stay in our place. The master never understood that we were people too, he just didn't give a dam. Night breeze.

87

Like Honey

Like honey she was sweet to the taste and sticky to the touch. Her golden appearance was thick and gooey, slow moving liquid reflecting the hypnotic motion grappling for my attention of separation once I engaged, I mesmerized at the point of being in awe of her as she captured my heart. There was no separation in the physicality of her substances. It was as though as if we merged as one. Her burnt yellowish color reflected my most inner desires. There was nothing more I've could have asked for. My eyes beheld her inner longing and craving to quench my thirst and hungry pains. Like honey dripping from a honeycomb slow and with purpose, I was destined to be the dip my fingers into the beehive of pleasure, the gold treasures of pure gold. Like honey.

88

Lovin Without Cost

Baby when it comes without cost. You ain't gotta pay for it. It's included in this of man. Package deal. No hidden fees. Baby, it's all free. My lovin is without cost of you having not to be perfect. You just gotta be the one that fits the criteria for getting all the benefits. But if you ain't drama free from gossiping, back biting and spreading rumors we may have some serious issues. These types of situations cost time that may incurred loss wages of hugs, some kissing, handholding with good-good caressing, morning, noon and night, because I'm hands on type of man. I can't waste precious time on nonsense. I wanna love without cost. When a man is loving his pleasure and not pain, therefore, woman it becomes it is all profit. Lovin without cost is when a woman allows a man to love without all the faking of going through the emotional roller-coasters rides. Relationships are only difficult when you create the wrong environment for them to grow and eventually it will die because it becomes too much work to handle. Lovin without cost.

89

Caught Between Two Worlds

Worlds colliding with one another. When one is not completely sure, confusion creeps in and creates a disorientating effect that leads to not being confident of the choices being made. Sometimes one can get stuck in the "Vallet of Indecisiveness." Should I or should I not, can take a toll on the psyche. One must make a choice about what they're willing to settle for before making a final decision of about accepting half of what they're looking for instead of the whole package deal. If that being the case, why do they always complain about it? The handwriting is on the wall of their heart if they take heed to the signs. One's intuitions will always tell you something wrong if you will only pay attention and listen. Caught between two worlds.

90

Alienation Love

The appearance of a stranger it appears to be, Unidentified touches without flush plush recognition of my mission is to come to turns about what is. I don't feel the bees love of honey like I used to because of all the abuse I've incurred over time. Seems like a mind-blowing situation goes south for an undetermined amount of time while the heart turns to strychnine blinded the toxic liquid love drink could turn pink. One must be careful how they engage into the domain of forbidden love. It could be good to you, but bad for the heart. Some relationships were never meant to be, but some people are high risk takers. It's all or nothing. They said you only live once. That may be true, but don't be "Coocoo for Coco puffs". If love is not a good fit and you try to force it, you'll end up with misery as your partner in crime. Alienation love.

91

Covenant or Contract

Is a covenant or a contract? Every time we get into a disagreement you threaten me with leaving. Did you forget at the alter the vows we made on that special day? Remember what you become, I mean covenant or contract? You see with a covenant the only way out if you die or at least that was the goal of getting married was I finally found someone worthy to give my body, souls and spirit to as one. This process can only happen once in one's lifetime once. On the other hand if it's a contract you break your covenant at ? will and make false state you can require ents to a multitude of individuals, repeating a vicious cycle of time something doesn't go your way you'll just get another person to take his or her place, To be in a covenant relationship you must be committed, Commitment is not concern with the other being perfect, it was already considered before the alter, before saying "I do". Commitment understands the challenges that might occur during this lifelong engagement, the one chosen by you. Contracts are simply rules that if you aren't fulfilled to the tee can require compensation for all the post-conceived losses of never being fully satisfied with the results of the other partner. The problem is they need to grow as one. Though they took the vows to become one, they never took place, it takes a lifetime to fulfill a covenant and only moments of unrealistic fantasies with a contract. Covenant or contract?

92

Play The Hand

Life can sometimes deal you a hand not to your liking. When life seems to go in the opposite direction don't panic, there's more than one way to reach your destiny. Don't worry about it when negative situations arise with contempt and want to dominate the narrative, the half ain't been told so don't go along with the negative flow. Play the hand that's delt to you, you never know what the outcome might be until you release what's in your hands. I've received some pretty bad hands when it came to relationships. Not all were good, not all were bad, but I still play with what's was before me. You live and learn a lot by engaging in different types of relationships. Sometimes you know really what you want until you get firsthand experiences about dealing with toxic situations. The key to playing the hand of relationships is to take your time. Too many times we rush into a relationship thinking you are in love when it's only infatuation. 4 Real love requires commitment. Commitment is not lead by emotions, because emotions are subject to change when things don't go your way. Some people like to play the relationship card only when it's in their favor, but that won't always be the case. If you play your cards right and take your time you can develop something special. Play the hand.

93

The Chameleon

Like a Chameleon her eyes changed with the disposition of her mood. Sometimes according to the encounter of life's unpredictable tests. Everyday seemed like a rollercoaster of ups and downs alluding to her perception of making complex choices to move forward with the unknown. When I saw green in her eyes meant every decision was made with an affirmative yes, meaning it was okay to proceed with safety. If the eyes changed to yellow it meant she was to move with caution because there was an element of the unknown, not having all the facts could be detrimental to the advancement of her intent. But if there was a red flashing signals warning her that eminent danger would pose a threat to her immediately safety was a clear indication, don't, do not, wait a minute, be very careful would be her saving grace to be aware. Often the answers would be yes, no and wait. Using her intuition to navigate life everyday issues was a must if she was to be successful in relationships. One who knew her could decipher her very moods by gazing into her eyes they were the very windows into her soul. The chameleon.

94

Face to Face

She caught a case where they had laced her coffin with traces of strychnine before she passed from this life to the next. She went from time to eternity. Face to face she stood before her Savior wondering if she had made it. She began to weep before the throne of GOD and the books were opened. Her name was called, she failed on her face and began to state her case. Every knee should bow, and every tongue shall confess. My sister had passed the test. She trembled with fear, Jesus threw nearby. Finally, she stood in the presences of her Savior because Jesus had labored to pay for her salvation. It was the revelation of Christ that made everything alright. She went from time to eternity where we will all see our Creator face to face where we will rejoice forever more. Have you met your GOD yet? Face to face.

95

Living In Exile

And she lived in exile fearing the loss of home, family and all the things she had known that is personal and dear. She was always having to hide from the public sector of being free to express one's opinions, views and voice to bring about change to enhance social change. She walked in the shadows of not being revealed to share her identity, not wanting to expose the sharing of bias words of condemnation. Always on the run from those with power changing her destiny. From freedom to bondage, from riches to poverty, from heaven to hell. Living exile is a life of imprisonment in a land of freedom. Living in exile.

96

I See with My Hands

I see with mt hands though I can feel the outer linings and texture that allow my senses to see on a more realistic level identifying what is before me. As I my hands glide down the surface of that which I'm in touching my fingertips send signal of imagery creating a visual picture that I began to comprehend the depths, the valleys, the hills and slops allowing my mind to form a picture of what I'm feeling. I instantly grasp the shapes, smooth, rough, soft and hard to recognize the differences in a world of variety. I see more with my hands more passionately than those who have the ability to see with vision. But to have both worlds one is truly fortunate. I see with mt hands.

Beyond

Beyond our thoughts are acts of passionately known through experiences of touching, holding, feeling, talking, caring, sharing and exchanging ideas, perceptions of one's own trues deemed to be of the purest form of truth within oneself.

Beyond our thoughts is a world filled with joys and happiness to be yet experienced through means of being present to know, to understand, to sense, to handle, to express your point of view as being a part of a greater revelation known to other than self.

Beyond you and I there is the agreement of two becoming one. Beyond.

Orange Love

Orange love is the sunniest of all intimate passions of sharing joys of feeling and reflecting the light of one's heart.

Orange love is the light that reveals the true inter reflection of revealing one's soulish desires for another.

Orange love are rays of hope for two engaged into the consenting travelers traveling the path of illumination.

Orange love is passion for lifetime given only for moments in time meant to last for eternity. Orange love.

99

Who Are You?

A question that everybody asks when life seems to transition them without permission. It's a question we sometimes can't always answer, and yet we seek to know and understand this finite journey of complication. It's ironic that we are not equipped with all the details necessary to make informed decisions that will propel us to the next level of primary truths set to make our way into the unknown place set before us. We tend not to ask questions to identify our real purpose for existing. So many times, we took out our first breath. Life is full of twists and turn, ins and outs, ups and downs. Sort of like a roller coaster highs and lows. Identity is the key to understanding where you originated are from whence you will finally arrive. Who are you is a question I ask myself often when life because dry and predictable. The when, the who's, the what's, and the where's becomes the point of reference to find my compass of hope. In part I understand to a degree of who I'm but there is so much more to what has already been revealed. I still ask the question who are you?

How Can You Say!

How can you say you love me when my nights are filled with uncertainty

How can you say you need me when I feel so all alone

How can you, how can I found mutual ground to love one another

For years I cried so many tears for so many years

For so many years I tried to overcome my fears I been lost in the sauce

I been fighting without a cause

But I remembered the cross the ultimate sacrifice for the lost

I saw the tears in your eyes I saw you were willing to die in my place

Even when I was the one who caught a case none could erase It was your love that took my place

It was not what you said, but you did on that special day in a special way

That said it all after my great fall being loved without boundaries has taken time to see about the legitimacy of your pure heart now I can see that your love went beyond the call of duty to set me free tried and true your love came out of the blue of true reality setting my soul aglow the fire that burns both day and night. How can you say!

Handwriting on The Wall

She saw it, she knew it, she ignored it. It was plain as daylight. Who could misinterpret that.

It was in a language she could understand, it was spelled out in colors, that meant no. Warning signs. And yet it seemed she didn't care. Her best friend told her that she was making a big m mistake. Don't do it. Others pleaded with her about being careful. There were "red flags" from the beginning of the relationship. Is that love or she is just infatuated? Handwriting on the wall is a tell-tale sign of trouble in the midst of a possible, dangerous relationship that could go south if there are no safety precautions taken. Sometimes people throw caution to the wind, knowing all too well there are risk to certain toxic relationships. And yet they're willing to take the chance, one cannot change a monster if a monster doesn't want to be changed. She was drawn that bad boy type. She loved the thug life type, to each her own. Everything comes with a price, a risk, a reward or consequence. Her choices would render deeds of her choosing. It's been said out everyone's heart will flow the issues of life that proceeds from thoughts. Handwriting on the wall.

Imprisoned

She was imprisoned by love with the notion that being questionable was freedom. But to her dismay the fictional cycle of separation was being in forced through excuses. I stood by only to observe this repeated cycle of half-love without commitment. Her heart was deeply ingrained into this game of hide and seek, a stealth lover under cover on a secret mission. I saw unconditional love in in its highest manifestation of giving without receiving. I asked myself how could a love so pure be stagnated without the emergence of real fruit? Real love flows without the influx of real fruit? Real love flows without restriction of fear, because perfect love cast out all fears. I'm amazed at the myriads of love affairs relays on the grounds of limitations of one party with two parts. Love is freedom not imprisonment. Love is the most difficult to find and the hardest of things to let go, Is true love really liberty ft bondage. Imprisonment,

www.ingramcontent.com/pod-product-compliance
Lightning Source LLC
LaVergne TN
LVHW051037070526
838201LV00010B/235